The INSIDE GUIDE

SPACE SCIENCE

Humans in Space

By Donna Reynolds

T0390589

Cavendish Square

Library of Congress Cataloging-in-Publication Data

Names: Reynolds, Donna, 1976- author.
Title: Humans in space / Donna Reynolds.
Description: Buffalo, NY : Cavendish Square Publishing, [2024] | Series:
The inside guide: space science | Includes bibliographical references
and index.
Identifiers: LCCN 2023025738 | ISBN 9781502670168 (library binding) | ISBN
9781502670151 (paperback) | ISBN 9781502670175 (ebook)
Subjects: LCSH: Astronautics–Juvenile literature. | Manned space
flight–Juvenile literature. | Space race–Juvenile literature. | Space
stations–Juvenile literature. | Outer space–Exploration–Juvenile
literature.
Classification: LCC TL793 .R455 2024 | DDC 629.45–dc23/eng/20230613
LC record available at https://lccn.loc.gov/2023025738

Editor: Jennifer Lombardo
Copyeditor: Jill Keppeler
Designer: Deanna Lepovich

Find us on

CONTENTS

Mars is one planet that can be seen from Earth without a telescope. In this picture, the moon is in the center, and Mars looks like a reddish star at the bottom right.

IN THE BEGINNING

For thousands of years, humans have studied the stars. Early civilizations used them to try to **predict** the future. Later, when tools such as the telescope were invented, scientists called astronomers began to study what was going on in space more closely. However, it wasn't until the 20th century that we were able to start sending objects and people into orbit.

Ancient Civilizations

Ancient civilizations made up myths, or stories, about what they saw in the sky. However, they also looked at space scientifically. Some ancient peoples were very advanced. Even without the tools we have today, they were able to use the movements of the sun, moon, planets, and stars to **accurately** keep time. The ancient Egyptians, Mesopotamians, and Maya all made calendars that helped them farm.

Fast Fact

Some people still believe that the position and movement of the stars and planets can tell the future or explain how people behave. This field of study is called astrology. It isn't a real science like astronomy.

The astrolabe (*shown here*) was invented by the Greeks about 225 BCE and improved by the Arabs in later years. It could be used to calculate the time of day and the time of sunrise and sunset, help with navigation, and more.

The ancient Greeks were one of the first civilizations to practice astronomy as a science, and they figured out many things that we know today are true. For example, a mathematician named Pythagoras realized about 500 BCE that Earth is round. However, the ancient Greeks were sometimes wrong. For instance, a great thinker named Aristotle thought Earth was the center of the universe.

Astronomy Takes Off

Between the 14th and 17th centuries CE, European astronomers started publishing books about what they had learned. Polish astronomer Nicolaus Copernicus's book *On the Revolutions of Heavenly Spheres* stated that the sun—not Earth—was the center of the solar system. Italian astronomer Galileo Galilei used telescopes to look into space and

Fast Fact

The Maya calendar was so advanced that scientists couldn't figure out exactly how it worked until 2023. That year, they realized the calendar keeps track of the planets' movements over a period of 45 years.

The invention of cameras with long exposure times allowed astronomers to take pictures of star trails. These appear because the stars stay still while Earth spins.

see things such as craters on the moon, spots on the sun, and an exploding star called a supernova.

Although telescopes helped move the field of astronomy forward, astronomers had many questions: What is the moon made of? What's outside our solar system? How big is the universe? These were things people would never know without seeing space up close. However, scientists knew that getting to space would take a lot of time, money, and hard work. They had to start small, using **technology** that already existed and improving it over time.

From Fireworks to Rockets

The ancient Chinese invented fireworks that were **propelled** by gunpowder. Although these were called rockets, they weren't used for space exploration. Some Chinese rockets were used in celebrations, while others were used as weapons.

When China began trading with other countries,

Without the Chinese, there would be no fireworks on the Fourth of July.

THE FATHERS OF ROCKETRY

The three men who studied rocket dynamics, or how rockets work, were Konstantin Tsiolkovsky of the Soviet Union, Hermann Oberth of Germany, and Robert Goddard of the United States. Through his work, Tsiolkovsky came up with a mathematical formula that is still used today to create spacecraft. This formula is named after him.

Oberth and Goddard each realized that a rocket would only be able to reach outer space if it used liquid fuel. Solid fuel, such as gunpowder, would take up too much space and weight because so much of it would be needed to overcome Earth's gravity. Many people doubted that liquid fuel could work, but Goddard proved it by building and testing the first liquid-fueled rocket engine.

Chinese people passed on the knowledge of how to make rockets. For many years, only armies used them. However, in the early 1900s, three men started studying how rockets worked and figured out ways to change them so the rockets could be used to send something—or someone—into space. None of the three men knew each other; they came up with their ideas independently around the same time period.

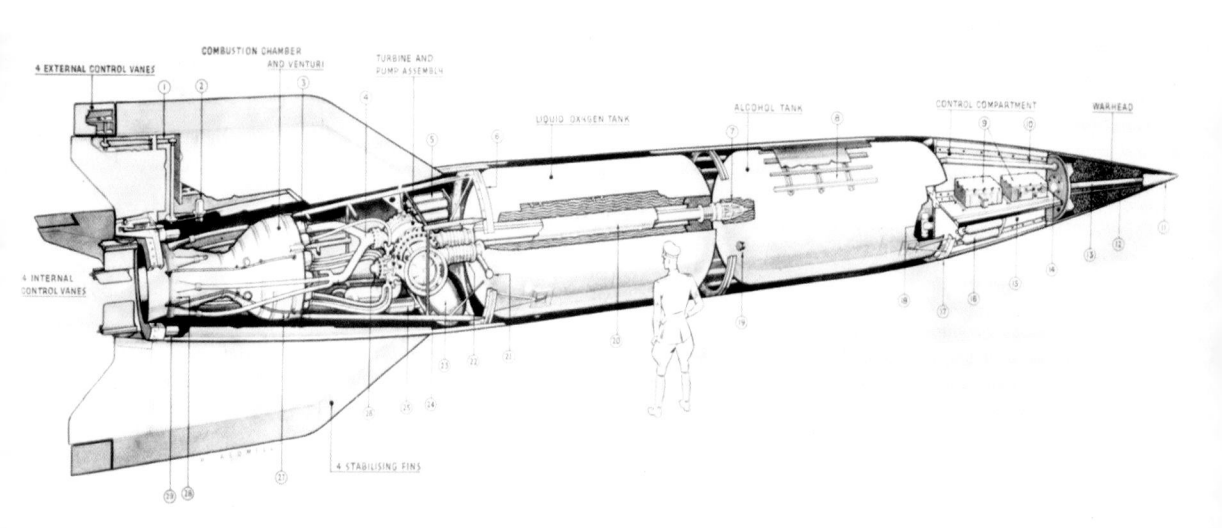

This picture shows what a German V-2 rocket looked like inside and out.

THE SPACE RACE

During World War II (1939–1945), German scientists worked on creating rockets—using enslaved Jews for labor—as weapons for Adolf Hitler and the Nazi Party. After the war, the United States brought some of these scientists to America to work on rockets for the U.S. Army. The Germans brought parts with them and rebuilt one of their rockets, which was called the V-2. On May 10, 1946, they launched a rocket 70 miles (112.7 kilometers) into the air.

Racing the Russians

Three days after the United States successfully launched the V-2, Joseph Stalin created a Soviet rocket program. At that time, Russia was the largest part of the Union of Soviet Socialist Republics (USSR), also called the Soviet Union. Stalin was the Soviet leader at that time.

The United States and USSR did not get along. Americans were worried that if the Soviets got to space

Fast Fact

The rebuilt V-2 was first launched on April 16, 1946. It only reached 3.4 miles (5.5 km) in the air before it flew off course and crashed. The rocket team made changes to the guidance, or steering, system before trying again in May.

HIDDEN FIGURES

The 2017 movie *Hidden Figures* shone a light on some of the Black female mathematicians who did the calculations necessary to make the U.S. rocket program successful.

first, they would control it. The U.S. government decided it was very important for the United States to get to space first and stop that from happening. This led to what is sometimes called the Space Race.

The United States had already been working on a rocket program. Their big lead on the Russians helped give Americans some early successes in the Space Race.

THE COLD WAR

From about 1947 to 1991, the United States and the USSR were involved in what is called the Cold War. Neither country trusted the other; each was worried the other would attack. To prevent this from happening, each country tried to show its military was the strongest.

The Space Race was part of the Cold War. Both the Americans and the Soviets believed that whoever could land a person on the moon first would be proven to have the best technology. If the Cold War hadn't happened, there would have been no need to rush, so it's likely that getting humans into space would have taken much longer than it did.

Unmanned and Manned

American and Soviet scientists worked tirelessly on their rocket programs, but it still took a long time. Without today's computers, all the calculations needed to be done by hand. The United States had an early success on September 20, 1956, when a rocket called the Jupiter-C flew higher, farther, and faster than any rocket before it.

The Soviets, not to be outdone, launched the first man-made **satellite** into orbit on October 4, 1957. The satellite, called *Sputnik 1*, completed 1,440 orbits of Earth before burning up in the atmosphere. *Sputnik 1* was an unmanned spacecraft, which means there were no living things on it. On November 3, 1957, the Soviets launched *Sputnik 2*, which held a three-year-old dog named Laika. This canine

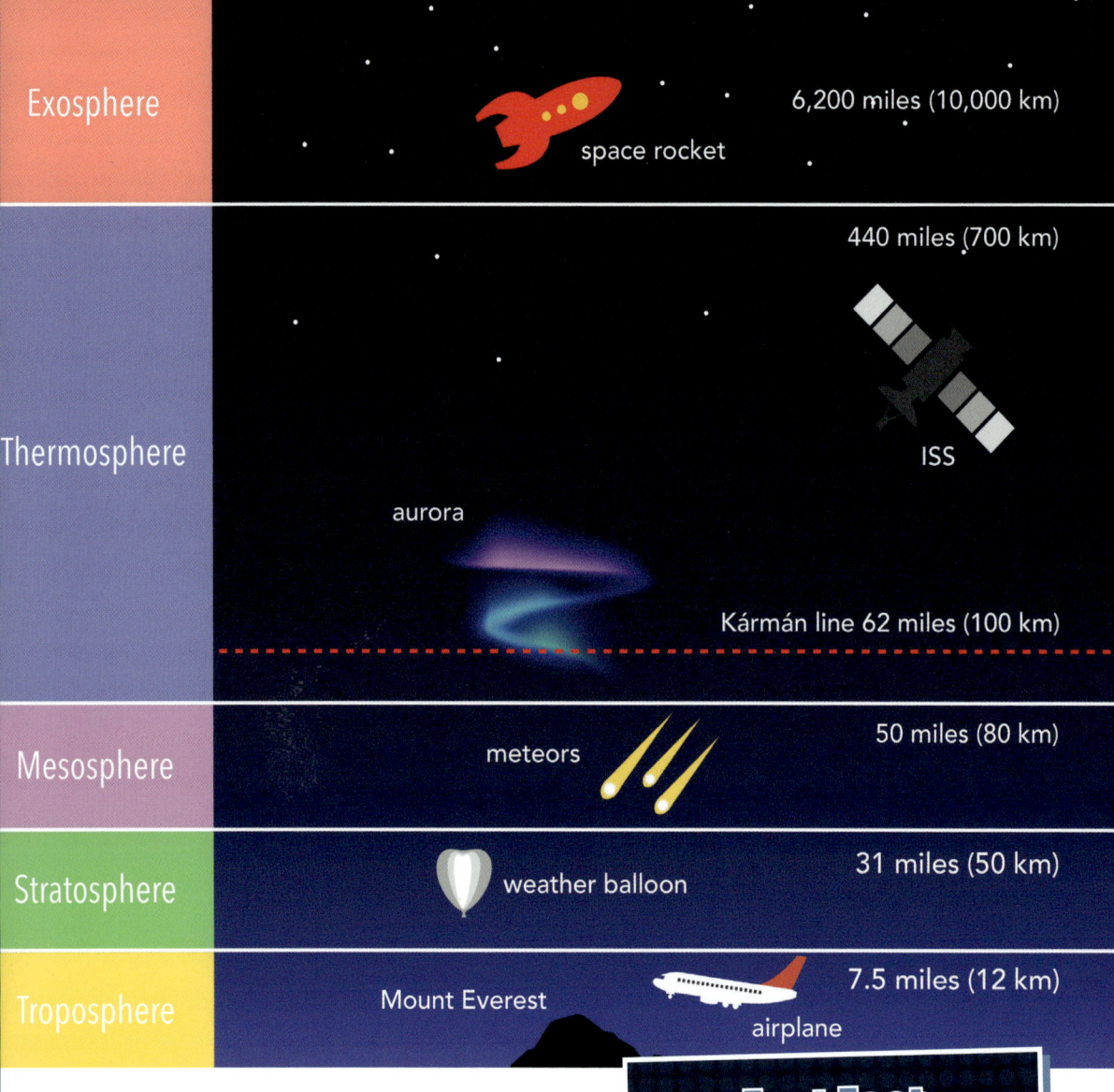

Exosphere	space rocket	6,200 miles (10,000 km)
Thermosphere	aurora / ISS	440 miles (700 km)
	Kármán line 62 miles (100 km)	
Mesosphere	meteors	50 miles (80 km)
Stratosphere	weather balloon	31 miles (50 km)
Troposphere	Mount Everest / airplane	7.5 miles (12 km)

This picture shows the layers of Earth's atmosphere. The Kármán line is where many countries consider that outer space starts. Spacecraft need to get past that point to go into orbit. If they don't reach it, they fall back to Earth.

Fast Fact

In the United States, only men were allowed to go into space until the 1980s, even though the U.S. space program couldn't have succeeded without women.

space traveler died after six hours, but the Soviets told everyone for many years that she had lived in space for four days.

The *Sputnik* launches pushed the Americans to create a manned space program that would be able to travel all the way to the moon. After a lot of research and many setbacks, including the deaths of several astronauts, the National Aeronautics and Space Administration (NASA) finally launched the Apollo 11 mission on July 16, 1969. It landed on the moon on July 20 and brought the astronauts home safely on July 24.

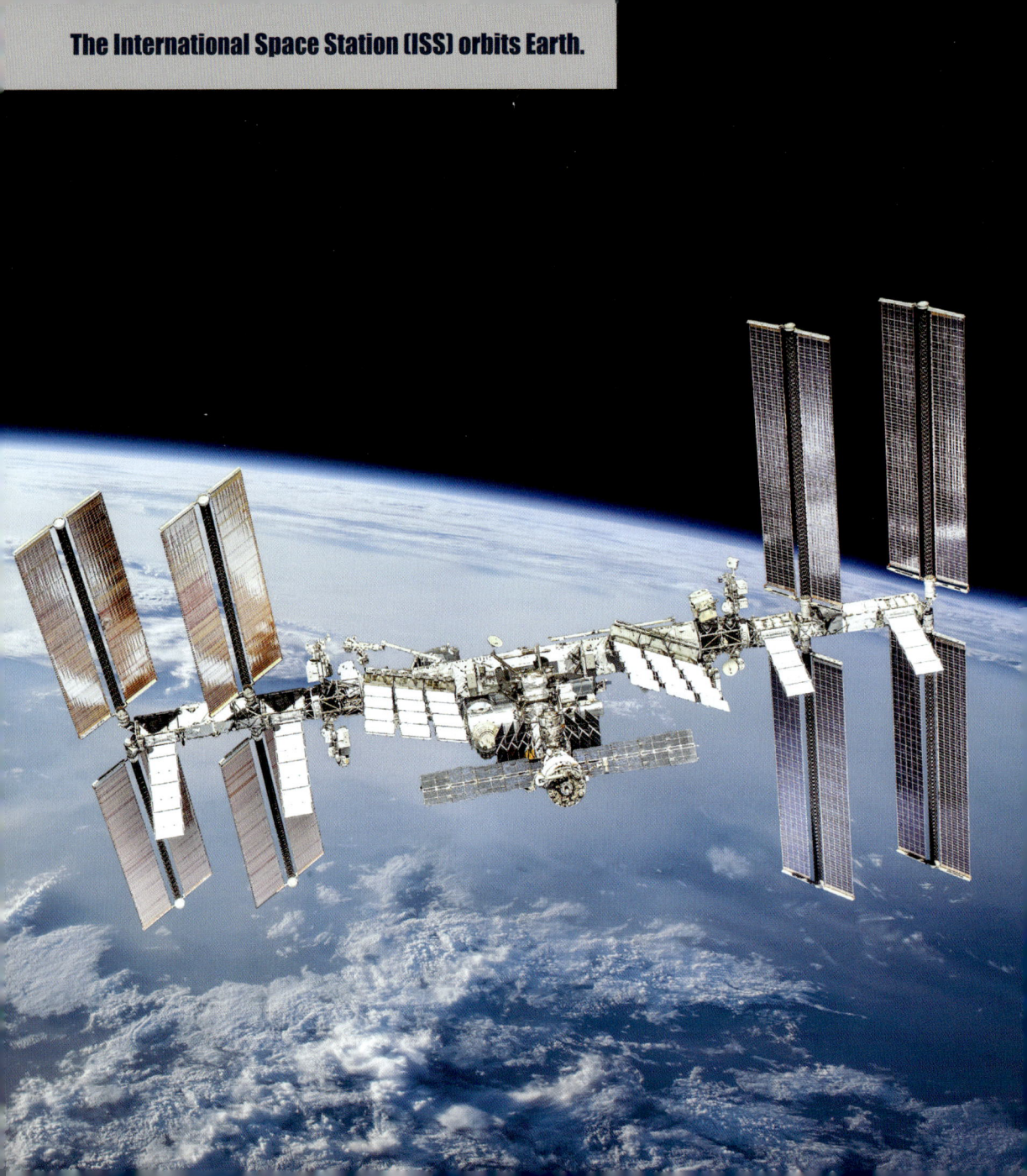

The International Space Station (ISS) orbits Earth.

Chapter Three

LIVING IN SPACE

The Soviets and Americans continued their space exploration even after the moon landing happened. In 1986, the Soviets started to build a space station called Mir. It was built in space a little at a time; the Soviets sent parts up and cosmonauts (the Russian word for astronauts) put them together. The cosmonauts lived on the space station while it was being assembled.

An End and a Beginning

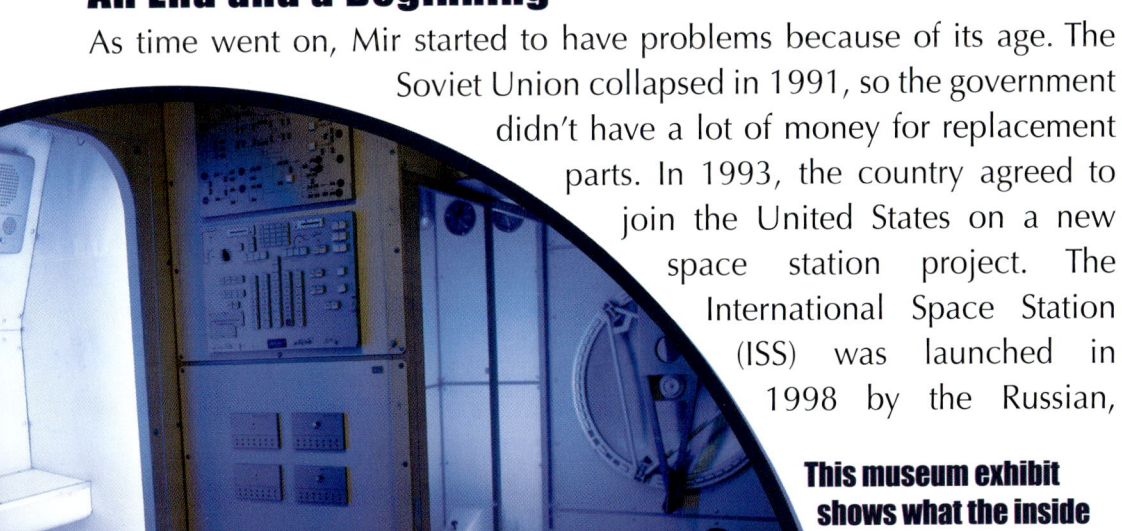

As time went on, Mir started to have problems because of its age. The Soviet Union collapsed in 1991, so the government didn't have a lot of money for replacement parts. In 1993, the country agreed to join the United States on a new space station project. The International Space Station (ISS) was launched in 1998 by the Russian,

This museum exhibit shows what the inside of Mir looked like.

U.S., European, Canadian, and Japanese space agencies.

Like Mir, the ISS was built in space a little at a time, and most construction was finished in 2012. However, astronauts have been living on it since 2000. Astronauts aren't just regular people who go to space for fun. They're trained scientists who use the ISS to do experiments that teach us more about how things work on Earth and in space.

The crew comes from many different countries, but the ISS is mostly controlled by the Russians and Americans. Each is in charge of half of the space station, although the crew doesn't live separately. In fact, a lot of cooperation is needed to keep the place running

Sometimes astronauts have to go outside the ISS to make repairs. When they do this, it's called a spacewalk.

SPACE TOURISM

In 2001, a man named Dennis Anthony Tito paid $20 million to stay a few days on the ISS, making him the world's first space tourist. Today, as technology improves, many companies are looking for ways to allow others to take space vacations. Companies such as SpaceX, Blue Origin, and more are working on short space flights.

As of 2023, some options are available, but the prices are much higher than most people can afford. For example, a company called World View offers a trip that lasts between 6 and 12 hours. Passengers sit in a space **capsule** attached to a large balloon, eat and drink, and look out the windows. One ticket costs $50,000.

smoothly. For this reason, the crew is trained to speak both English and Russian.

Life in Space

Adjusting to life in space can be hard because of the absence of gravity. Things that are easy to do without a second thought on Earth take more time and effort in space. One of the biggest adjustments to zero gravity is maintaining the body. Without Earth's gravity, the human body doesn't work right on its own. For example, if you hold your arm in the air on Earth, it will get tired quickly because your muscles are pushing against gravity. In space, the muscles don't have to do any work. Astronauts are required to do two hours of exercise every day so their muscles and bones don't break down.

Another challenge is conserving water. Astronauts can't just turn on a faucet or go outside to get water. This means all liquid—including sweat and pee—is collected, recycled, and cleaned. This turns it into water that can be used for drinking and showering. Washing clothes is impossible; instead, when clothes are too dirty to be worn anymore,

Being underwater is the closest people can get to zero gravity on Earth. For this reason, astronauts practice doing tasks underwater so they know how to do them in space.

astronauts put them in a one-time-use spacecraft and launch it from the ISS. It burns up in Earth's atmosphere, so from the ground, it looks like a shooting star.

Even sleeping is difficult on the ISS! Astronauts have to attach their sleeping bags to the wall so they don't float around. They also have to schedule their sleep times. As the ISS orbits Earth, it sees 16 sunrises and sunsets every 24 hours. Since astronauts can't rely on the sun to tell them when it's night or day, they schedule 8 hours of sleep and set an alarm so they know when it's time to wake up.

The ISS has windows so astronauts can look out into space. The bright spot on the planet is a flash of lightning.

NASA has created a special rocket called the Space Launch System (SLS) rocket that's powerful enough to carry astronauts and all their equipment to the moon.

TO THE MOON AND BEYOND

Humans haven't been back to the moon since the 1970s, but NASA is working on changing that with an ongoing project called Artemis. The goal is to set up a space station called Gateway near the moon as well as a permanent settlement on the surface.

Gateway will have two functions. The first will be to give astronauts a place to live as they study the moon. Some astronauts will stay on the space station while others live on the moon. The second

Gateway isn't built yet, but this picture shows what it's meant to look like.

Fast Fact

The first moon project was called Apollo after the Greek god of the sun. In Greek mythology, Artemis, his twin sister, is the goddess of the moon.

function will be to give spacecraft a place to stop and stock up on fuel and supplies before continuing to other places, such as Mars.

Exploring Mars

A huge goal for many of the world's space programs and private space exploration companies is to send a manned mission to Mars. NASA has already sent several **rovers** to Mars to take pictures and samples. These rovers have taught us a lot about Mars. For example, by **analyzing** samples of the dirt, the rovers were able to break down what's in it. This is how we know that Mars looks red because it has oxidized, or rusty, iron in its dirt.

Because going to space is dangerous, or unsafe, astronauts have to do a lot more testing before humans can be sent to Mars or even just to the moon for a long period of time. If something goes wrong in space, help is a long way away; there are no doctors or firefighters who can get there quickly. For this reason, NASA doesn't expect to send out a manned mission to Mars until at least 2030.

Exoplanets

In the very distant future, scientists hope to send people to exoplanets, or planets outside our solar system. They're especially interested in finding another planet where humans can live comfortably. This would be a

Fast Fact

Before going to Mars, NASA plans to send manned missions around the moon by 2024 and to an asteroid by 2025. This timeline may get pushed back if problems come up.

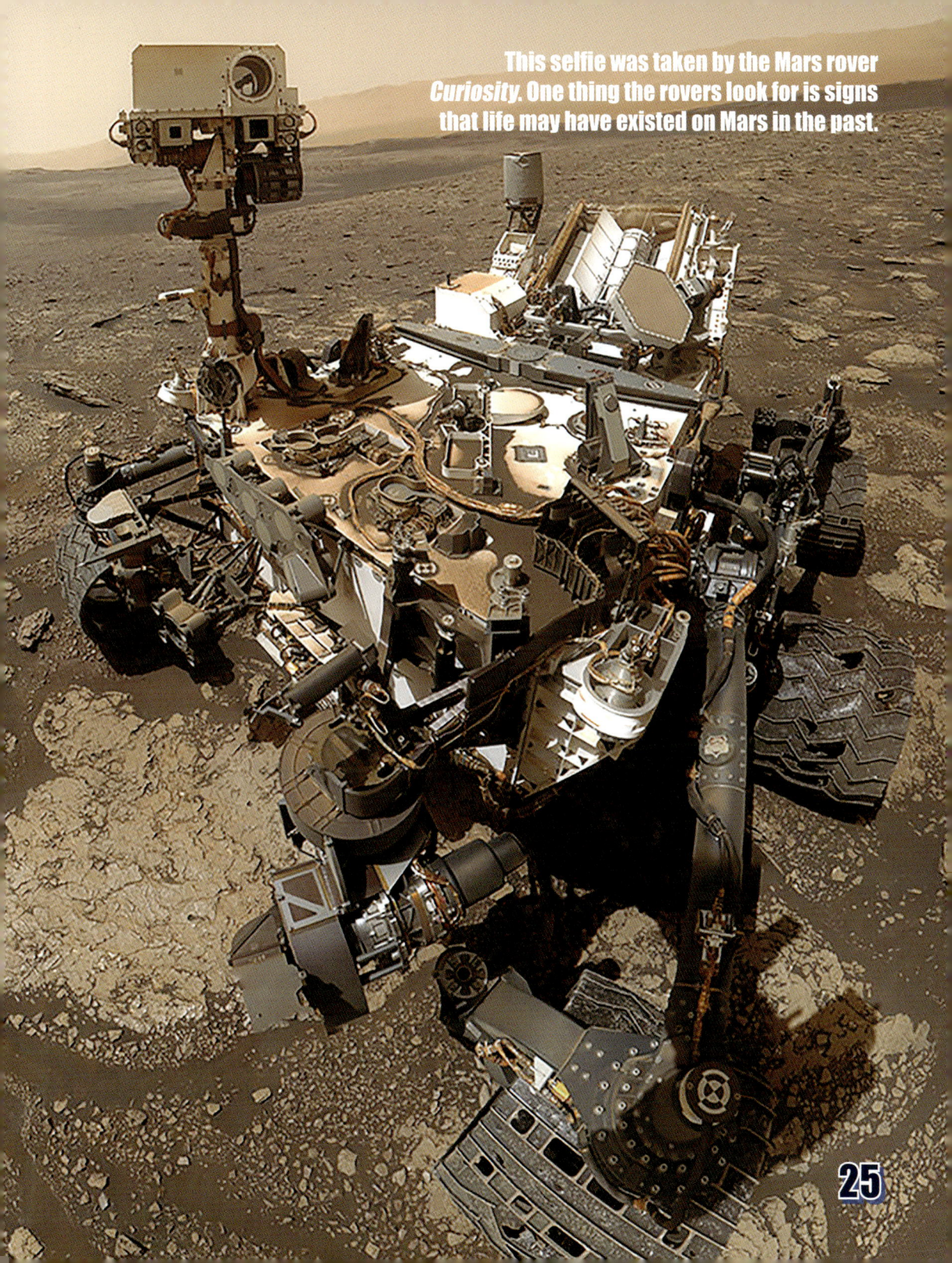

This selfie was taken by the Mars rover *Curiosity*. One thing the rovers look for is signs that life may have existed on Mars in the past.

WHY GO BACK?

Scientists want to go back to the moon for several reasons. One is to practice going on longer trips—first to Mars, and eventually outside the solar system. Any problems that come up can be fixed while the spacecraft is still fairly close to Earth.

Another reason is learning more about the moon and Earth, such as how they first formed. NASA has also stated building a moon base will give people more jobs on Earth and in space, allowing the **economy** to grow. Some people are excited about Project Artemis. Others believe it's a waste of money.

Fast Fact

A light-year is a measure of distance, not time. It's the distance light travels in one Earth year. Light moves so fast that it's impossible for anything to match its speed.

very long and dangerous journey, and no space program is anywhere near ready to take it on. The closest exoplanet we know of is Proxima Centauri b, which orbits the star Proxima Centauri. The planet is 4.2 light-years away. With the technology we have right now, it would take about 6,300 years to get there!

If humans were to travel to Proxima Centauri b, the spaceship would need to be like a traveling village. Whole generations

This drawing shows one idea of what a base on the moon or an exoplanet might look like.

would be born and die on the spaceship, never touching either planet. We simply don't have the technology to do that right now, but as scientists continue to work on the problem, humans may one day live their whole lives in space.

1. Why do you think we can't see star trails without a camera?

2. How do you think history might be different if the Soviets had gotten to the moon first?

3. What other ways do you think a lack of gravity affects the way people live in space?

4. What problems can you think of that might come up on a long space journey?

GLOSSARY

accurately: In an accurate manner, or free from mistakes.

analyze: To study closely, especially to determine the relationship of separate parts.

capsule: A small compartment with nearly normal atmospheric pressure for a pilot or astronaut.

economy: The way goods and services are made and sold.

exposure: In cameras, the length of time the shutter stays open when taking a single photo.

osteoporosis: A disease that causes loss of bone density, making bones more likely to break.

predict: To figure out in advance.

propel: To move forward.

rover: A machine built to explore the surface of a moon or another planet.

satellite: A man-made object or vehicle intended to orbit Earth, the moon, or another heavenly body.

technology: Using science to solve problems; also, the equipment used to solve those problems.

FIND OUT MORE

Books

Hubbard, Ben. *The Complete Guide to Space Exploration: A Journey of Discovery Across the Universe*. Victoria, Australia: Lonely Planet Global Limited, 2020.

Szymnanski, Jennifer. *Space Exploration*. New York, NY: Children's Press, 2021.

Websites

BrainPOP: Space Flight
www.brainpop.com/technology/scienceandindustry/spaceflight
Watch a movie, play games, and take a quiz to test your knowledge of space flight.

NASA: Exoplanet Exploration
exoplanets.nasa.gov
Discover planets outside our solar system, and learn whether humans might someday reach them.

NASA Space Place
spaceplace.nasa.gov
Find out more about what NASA has learned through decades of space exploration.

INDEX